TAO TE CHING

by Lao Tzu

A twenty-first century English interpretation

by

Jerome

I0173215

𝒮

STANSBURY
PUBLISHING
Chico, Ca.

TAO TE CHING
by Lao Tzu

A twenty-first century English interpretation
by
Jerome

Copyright © 2016, 2020 by Jerome Dirnberger
First edition 2016, Second edition 2020

ISBN   978-1-935807-51-3 2nd ed. pbk.
       978-1-935807-19-3 1st ed. pbk.
       978-1-935807-20-9 ePub
       978-1-935807-21-6 Kindle

Library of Congress Control Number 2016936955
Second Edition

Stansbury Publishing is an imprint of
Heidelberg Graphics

YIN-YANG CIRCLE AND TIME

The Chinese have a symbol which has enchanted me ever since I read about it in *The Faith of Other Men* (W. C. Smith). It is the Yin-Yang Circle.

"Take a circle, and divide it in two equal and congruent parts by drawing an S-shaped curve from top to bottom so that you have two, as it were, curved tear-drops nesting one against the other. One should be black and the other white. Put a dot of white in the middle of the largest bulbness part of the black, and a black dot in the white; suggesting that each half of the circle lightly touches or invades the other. You are left with a perfectly symmetrical figure such that you cannot say whether it is a black circle with a graceful white tear-drop in it, or a white circle with a graceful black tear-drop, or two contrasting tear-drops so inter-posed as to constitute together a perfect whole, flawlessly circular, or a perfect circle divided into two equal, contrasting, inter-penetrating, and lovely parts. With its total balance, and its endless, sinuous curves, it is a superb synthesis of rest and movement, of contrast and concord, of immediacy and ultimacy."

This symbol is an insight into my theological philosophy. Yang and Yin are fundamental principles explaining matter, events, philosophy—the whole cosmos. *Yang* is heat (fire), light, dry, movement, war, masculinity; while *Yin* is cold, dark, moist, rest, peace, femininity. Nothing exist or happens (that can be explained) without this dichotomy. They contrast but yet they blend into an unity. In fact it is impossible to conceive of one without the other. Man-Body & Soul

I would like to add another dimension to the yin-yang circle—to view it as a sphere. This added dimension adds a "time" element. Not however a static one—rather a dynamic one because a sphere has the greatest mobility of all physical objects by the fact that it does not have any "level" (flat) sides.

Time moves continually
    it cannot stand still

it has to be dynamic
    it is continually progressing
        time cannot stop.

I am referring or trying to describe time in a historical perspective rather than analyzing it, i.e. scientifically or philosophically. Yet as the sphere rolls forward, it can be observed that it will repeat itself. (For example, paint a white spot on a black ball and roll it. The white spot repeats its action cyclically.) So my time concept is not purely linear nor cyclic. Time moves forward repeating itself in a sense. Historical events are unique because they involve unique historical men—yet history does repeat itself: war and peace, good and bad economic times, growth and decline, etc.

Man alternates between conflict and peace, depression and elation, sorrow and joy, despair and hope, hate and love, dishonesty and truth, selfishness and selflessness. History is made by man. Man is *yin-yang*.

Jerome
10-8-67

PREFACE

My first published article was in a Jesuit magazine in the early 1960s. After I left the Society of Jesus, I received a BA from the University of Notre Dame concentrating my studies in early Christianity. I went on to do graduate studies in cultural anthropology at the University of Colorado. While my professional career has been in business, I continued my interests in comparative religions and religious philosophy including publishing *The Writings of Jerome*, *Thinking Critically to Develop a Philosophy of Life*, and *The Gospel of Thomas: The Original Sayings of Jesus*.

I started reading the *Tao Te Ching* a few years ago and realized it was almost identical to my philosophy that I had evolved over my life's journey. I studied many translations and interpretations none of which were easily understood without commentaries. I decided to write my own for me. Then it occurred maybe I should let others enjoy my efforts. If you wish to contact me, my email address is jadirnberger@gmail.com.

—Jerome Dirnberger

INTRODUCTION

TAO TE CHING (dow deh jing) can be translated as Book (Ching) of the Way (Tao), chapters 1–37, and Virtue (Te), chapters 38–81. It was written over twenty-five hundred years ago by Lao Tzu who is known as an "archivist for a Chinese kingdom." Lao Tzu is translated to mean "Old Master" and is not a proper name.

This publication is an interpretation not a translation. It is my interpretation. There are many other versions of *Tao Te Ching* written. The original uses images and concepts that can have several meanings as language has changed over the centuries. I am trying to accurately interpret the original ideas, but it is up to the reader to ponder my interpretations and draw his or her own conclusions. An exercise I recommend is writing your own *Tao Te Ching*. The purpose of my work is to stimulate critical thinking.

— *Jerome*

TAO TE CHING #1

Man cannot comprehend the depth of
The Creator nor Her creation
A universe of matter and energy

Man cannot fully understand how
The physical laws regulate
The relationship of matter and energy

Forget trying to be rational
And your mind will expand
Then you might perceive reality

Become aware of your part in the universe
Understand the *Tao* within you
Then you might perceive the right path

TAO TE CHING #2

When a person knows beauty
    She also knows ugly
When a person knows good
    She also knows evil

Existence and nonexistence create each other
Difficult and easy balance each other
Long and short define each other
High and low attract each other
Pitch and tone harmonize each other
Past and future follow each other

So a Taoist actions speak for herself
Her example teaches without explanation
She thinks but does not possess ideas
She does not demand expectations of others
She is successful when others take credit

TAO TE CHING #3

A Taoist society does not put people on a pedestal
    So there is no discord
A Taoist society does not treasure objects
    So there are no thieves
A Taoist society does not focus on unrealistic
  desires
    So there is no confusion about ethics

A Taoist leader leads by example with
    An open mind with no biases
    A strong belief in the natural order
    A conviction that moderation is a way of life
    A moral character of respect for everyone

Thus a Taoist people live in peace
So the society progresses into greater harmony
And the people are patient with how events evolve

TAO TE CHING #4

The Tao is like a black hole
Difficult to fully comprehend
It seems empty but it has purpose
Maybe the beginning of the next Big Bang

The Tao permeates the natural order
It balances extremes
It makes easy the path
It brings everything into harmony

The Tao is profound
It is eternal
It is the thought before creation
Do you think it has a pre-existence?

TAO TE CHING #5

The Tao is not biased
It treats every thing impartially
A Taoist is not biased
It treats every one impartially

The space between heaven and earth
Is like a bellows
While the air seems empty
It is inexhaustible
The more it pumps
The more air it produces
A concept difficult to understand
The same as understanding the Tao in you

TAO TE CHING #6

The universe (*Tao*) is like a great valley
Seemingly endless and serene
Yet She gives birth to many worlds

A Taoist understands this balance
Of creating and tranquility

TAO TE CHING #7

Before heaven and earth exist
There was the *Tao*, eternal and infinite
Energy and matter do not exist for themselves
Therefore they will endure

A Taoist does not exist for herself
She embraces benevolence and humility
Thus in being selfless, she succeeds

TAO TE CHING #8

Strive to do good
For goodness is like water
It nourishes without even trying
It is content to lie in lowly places
Thus it mirrors the *Tao*

So at home, be grounded
In thinking, be critical
With others, be generous and compassionate
When you speak, be sincere
As a leader, do not control
When working, enjoy it
With your family, give of yourself

So when you are content with yourself
You do not need to compete nor compare
Thus you earn respect

TAO TE CHING #9

If you do too much
You end up doing nothing
If you sharpen a blade too long
You dull it
If you seek riches
Your quest never ends
If you are proud of your achievements
You become arrogant

Follow the *Tao* as best you can
So when the path ends
You pass on peacefully

TAO TE CHING #10

In understanding your personal y*in* and *yang*
    Can you balance them?
In focusing your *ch'i*
    Can it be as plaint as a newborn's?
In clearing your mind
    Can it be free of distractions?
In being a government leader
    Can it be done free of military influence?
In dealing with the cycles of nature
    Can you be patient?
In being intellectually open
    Can you be objective?

Be productive
Nourish others
Do not be possessive
Act without expectations
Evolve without controlling
These are the powers of Virtue (*Te*)

TAO TE CHING #11

When thirty spokes meet at the wheel's axis
The center space makes the wheel useful,
When you form clay into a cup
The center space gives it utility
When you frame doors and windows for a house
The openings make the home comfortable
Therefore, purpose comes from not what is there
But because of what is not there

TAO TE CHING #12

The five colors can blind
The five tones can deafen
The five tastes can numb
Greedy actions weaken the mind
Uncontrollable desires destroy the will

The Taoist rejects the material world
To experience harmony with her inner self

TAO TE CHING #13

Be aware of both success and failure
Both faith and fear are selfish

What does it mean to 'be aware of both success
    and failure'
Success builds up your ego
While failure makes you insecure
Either one makes you unstable
Only when you can balance their effects
Can you stand on solid ground emotionally

What does it mean that 'both faith and fear are
    selfish'
They are in your imagination, they are deceptive
So the basis of your fear is selfish
Only when you are selfless, is there nothing to
    fear

When you understand your part in the universe
Will you act in harmony
When you love your part in the universe
Will you live in harmony

TAO TE CHING #14

Look, yet you cannot see
Listen, yet you cannot hear
Touch, yet you cannot feel
These three concepts merged together
Cannot be understood by ordinary men

How can the sun rise but not be bright?
How can the sun set yet not be dark?
How do you name nothing?
How do you describe formless?

So the *Tao* is called
A formless form
An image of nothing
A thought beyond comprehension

Understand in the beginning there was no end
So the unknowable can be known
If you learn to be aware of yourself and
Realize where you came from
This is the beginning of real wisdom (*Tao*)

TAO TE CHING #15

The wisdom of the Tao Master is profound
While difficult to describe
One can see it in her actions

Careful as one walks over thin ice
Aware as one in enemy territory
Courteous as a guest
Fluid as melting ice
Simple as a block of wood
Open like a valley
Candid as a child
Patient as mud settles in water
Intuitive in waiting for the right moment

The Tao Master does not possess power
She wants only to be a conduit for its energy (*chi*)
The more she gives, the more she acquires

TAO TE CHING #16

Set your mind at rest
Find peace in your heart
So you realize you are apart of every living thing
In doing this you understand the cycles of life

Each living thing while separate is apart of the
    Creator
Its destiny is to return to the Creator
Where it will experience serenity

This cycle is the source of the *Tao*
To realize this is to be insightful
If you do not, you become confused

To know the way of the *Tao* is to be tolerant
What is tolerant is unbiased
What is unbiased is influential
What is influential is dignified
What is dignified is the *Tao*

To be one with the *Tao* is to abide forever
You can deal with life's cycles
And when death comes, you are ready

TAO TE CHING #17

The Tao leader governs the citizens
Who barely recognize his guiding influence
The next best leader is one who is loved
Below him is one who is feared
The worst is one who is despised

If a leader does not trust the citizens
Then they will not trust him

So the Tao leader does not just make speeches
His actions are his leadership style
His success comes when the people say
"We freely govern ourselves."

TAO TE CHING #18

When the people lose their Way (*Tao*)
By not being compassionate and respectful
They become self-righteous
The corrupted become hypocrites
The family becomes less harmonious
The arrogant show off their piety

The whole nation becomes confused
Isolationism emerges

TAO TE CHING #19

Eliminate boastful wisdom
Abandon deceptive morality
The people are a hundred times better off
Eliminate arrogance
Abandon gratuitous benevolence
Families will be united in harmonious love
Eliminate devious righteousness
Abandon selfish profit
Thieves will no longer exist

These ways of civilized behavior
May not be enough

To follow the Tao
Perceive integrity
Embrace simplicity
Reduce egoism
Limit desires

TAO TE CHING #20

Is a university education better
    Than life's experiences?
Is saying "yes, sir" better
    Than saying "yeah, sure"?
Is your good my evil
    Or my good your evil?
Are the things you fear
    The same as those I fear?

Most people like parades and travel
    I prefer quiet and solitude
Most people like to shop
    I prefer to take a hike
Most people watch TV
    I prefer to read a book
Most people love to party
    I prefer to meditate
Most people need religion
    I prefer to be critical

I am open like a child
I am restless like the ocean
I am penetrating like the wind
I am rebellious in my thinking
I get my energy from the Tao

TAO TE CHING #21

Before time and space
The *Tao* is
But what is the *Tao*?

It is found in your unconsciousness
It is found in your awareness
It is found in the laws of nature
It is found in reality

Before matter and energy
The *Tao* is

How do I know this truth
Because the *Tao* is in me

TAO TE CHING #22

To succeed, first experience failure
To follow a straight path, first follow crooked ones
To be rich, be poor first
To be wise, learn first to be young

If you want everything, give up everything
Yet if you have much, you will be confused

The Taoist's actions speak for herself
Because she is not arrogant, she is respected
Because she does not judge, she is an example
Because she does not boast, she is trusted
Because she does not aggrandize, she is accepted
Because she does not compete, she is not
    challenged

So the old saying of "if you want everything, give
    up everything"
Is not just words, rather it is at
The heart of the *Tao*

TAO TE CHING #23

Nature is rarely aggressive
But when it is
Like a tornado lasting a few minutes
Or a thunderstorm for a few hours
How can man be more powerful?

A Taoist who is faithful to the *Tao*
She identifies with the natural order
And her insights show it

A Taoist who cultivates her personal strength (*Te*)
Knows it brings her harmony and freedom
And her attitude shows it

So men who fail to recognize this reality
Are seen as lacking in respect for others
And live confused lives

Men who lack belief
Will not be believed

TAO TE CHING #24

He who is arrogant does not judge fairly
He who is a hypocrite cannot be moral in his
    actions
He who is conceited is not esteemed by others
He who is full of pride is not respected by the
    meek
He who is aggressive will be over-powered
    himself
He who is boastful only speaks hollow words

Hence a Taoist does not do these things
A Taoist acts with humility and simplicity

TAO TE CHING #25

Before the universe was born
There was something…infinite

Something serene, independent, unchanging,
Eternal, vast…it is the mother of the universe
For lack of a better name…I call it *TAO*
The *Tao* flows through all things…inside,
Outside, and returns to the beginning

The *Tao* is Great
The universe is Great
Earth is Great
Mankind is Great
These are the four Great powers

Mankind follows the laws of the earth
The earth follows the laws of the universe
The universe follows the laws of the *Tao*
The *Tao* follows itself…the natural laws

TAO TE CHING #26

Consider a society like a giant tree
The trunk is grounded and unmoving
While the branches move with the wind

A great leader is like the trunk
The people are the branches
She is grounded providing subsistence
She is stable no matter the elements

She is serene within herself
She accepts her purpose

TAO TE CHING #27

A good hiker leaves no footprints
A good artist follows her intuition
A good scientist keeps an open mind
Yet a good lock cannot be opened
And a good knot cannot be unfastened

A Taoist is open to all
    So no one person is rejected
Plus all things are utilized
    So nothing is wasted

This is called "following your inner light"

Sometimes a good person teaches a bad person
And yet this bad person is a good resource

If you do not understand this,
    You are likely to get lost along the Way,
    No matter how intelligent you are

This is one of the great secrets of the *Tao*

TAO TE CHING #28

Understand male attributes
But emphasize the female ones
Be open to the world
Like streams that fill the rivers
Be open like a young child
Then the *Te* will be in you

Understand the white side of things
But practice the black side
Be aware of various cultures
So you can lead by example
Then the *Te* will be in you

Understand the rich and powerful
But act with humility and simplicity
Like a valley filled from different sources
Then the *Te* will be in you

Disperse your *Te* to create *ch'i*
Like a carpenter forms with little waste
Many utensils from a block of wood
In this way the *Tao* is known

TAO TE CHING #29

Do you want to change the planet?
I do not think you can succeed

Treat the planet as a sacred vessel
It is for too complicated for man to comprehend
If you try to change it, you will ruin it
If you treat it irreverently, you will lose it

There is a time to lead, and a time to follow
There is a time to act, and a time to rest
There is a time for things to grow, and a time of
    decay
There is a time to advance, and a time to retreat

The Taoist understands all this and
    Avoids extremes
    Avoids excesses
    Avoids extravagances

TAO TE CHING #30

Tao leaders do not desire to use force
Believing it results in force being returned

The Tao leader knows of the tremendous costs
Of maintaining a large army
Even that future generations have to pay the price

The Tao leader knows of other options
To achieving his goals
Rather than using force

To achieve goals the Tao leader
    Cannot be boastful
    Cannot be proud
    Cannot be arrogant
    Cannot be greedy

Following the Tao brings about peace that lasts
What is contrary to the Tao brings about
    devastating war

TAO TE CHING #31

Weapons of war never bring good fortune
They should be used as a last resort
Or better avoided at all costs
But if compelled great restraint is a must

Praising a victory shows disrespect for
All the common people on both sides
Who were injured or died
A Taoist leader does not rejoice in others' suffering

Tradition says on happy occasions you stand on
    the left
On sad occasions you stand on the right side
Plus civilian leaders should be on the left
And military commanders on the right side
So does that mean war is on par with funerals?
In truth all survivors should mourn all the dead
And admit that victories are really funerals

TAO TE CHING #32

Man will never fully understand the Universe
Even the smallest known particle
Contains galaxies

If company leaders understood the Tao
They would operate their companies simply
They would allow their employees to be creative
They would encourage teamwork and delegation

When companies are started
Many controls, rules, and regulations are
    established
But a Tao leader knows when enough is enough

A Tao company should be like gentle streams
Flowing into rivers on their way to the ocean

TAO TE CHING #33

To know others is clever
To know yourself is insightful
To control others is powerful
To control yourself is strong-willed

Those who know when enough is enough are
    wealthy
Those who are true to the *Tao* are determined
So when they die, they do not perish

TAO TE CHING #34

The Tao's force permeates the universe
Everything depends on it for sustenance
It denies nothing nor no one
Yet it does not act like a master
Its purpose is to let everything flow
Along the natural order

A Taoist has no desire for personal rewards
Taoists do not seek greatness
Their preferred goal is harmony

TAO TE CHING #35

The Taoist perspective of the universe
Brings her peace, security, and serenity

While music and food may satisfy
A person for a brief time
Seemingly unclear and monotonous
Words of Tao will endure

TAO TE CHING #36

In the end a company will shrink
    When previously it had over-extended
In the end a company will shed employees
    When before it had expanded too fast
In the end a company will lose income
    When before it had excessive profits
In the end a company's products will decline
    When before they were popular

This is the subtle wisdom of business cycles
When a company is seemingly strong, it will then
    weaken
When a company is too bureaucratic, it will
    become inflexible

Like it is wrong to take a fish out of water
A company should always be adaptable
Remember excessiveness produces decline

TAO TE CHING #37

The eternal *Tao* is harmony
In the natural order

If the rulers of men
Could grasp its *chi*
The world would be transformed
By calmness and tranquility
The people would be content
In their simple daily life
Free of excessive desires

There would be peace

TAO TE CHING #38

A Taoist does not seek to be influential
Thus he is
A man who seeks power
Never has enough
A man who is always doing something
Ends up doing nothing

A Taoist man follows the natural order
By not acting to control
A compassionate man acts intuitively
And does so without motivation
A just man thinks before acting
And has ulterior motives
A religious man takes premeditative action
Yet when no one follows
He resorts to force

A person who does not comprehend the Tao
    Sees only the external façade
    And begins his journey of delusion

Therefore a Taoist
    Prefers substance to superficial
    Dwells in the fruit not in the flower
    Embraces what is within not what is without

TAO TE CHING #39

When our planet is in harmony with the Tao
The sky is clear
The land is fertile
Living things are abundant
Streams run full
All creatures reproduce
Even rulers are compassionate

When man is not in harmony with the Tao
The sky becomes polluted
The land is barren
Living things die off
Streams dry up
Many creatures become extinct
Rulers are corrupt and greedy

Truly humility is the root for greatness
Rulers are successful when the people are
They are not arrogant nor boastful
They attain honor without being honored

TAO TE CHING #40

Adapt to the endless cycles of the *Tao*
    Like birth and death
    Like *yin* and *yang*
    Like active and passive

All things are created by energy (*chi*)
And yet energy was produced from nonexistence

TAO TE CHING #41

When a great leader hears about the Tao
    He diligently tries to understand all
When an average leader hears of the Tao
    He believes some ideas but doubts others
When a foolish leader hears of the Tao
    He roars with laughter

Ironically, if he did not laugh
    It would not be the Tao

Thus a Tao Master has said:
Acquiring insights seems difficult
One step forward seems to be two steps back
The right path seems to be the wrong way

On your path of Tao
Your personal power (*Te*) seems weak
Your morality seems questionable
Your will seems insufficient
Your vision seems obscure
Your understanding seems confused

Sometimes the greatest art seems so simple
The greatest wisdom seems childish
The greatest talents are slowly learned

Remember the Tao is formless and nameless
Yet it nourishes and completes all things

TAO TE CHING #42

The TAO produced ONE (space and time)
ONE produced TWO (positive and negative [*yin & yang*])
TWO produced THREE (matter, energy, natural law)
THREE produced everything in the universe

Everything carries *yin* and holds *yang*
So each thing is connected and dependent on everything
Thus one thing's gain is another's loss
And one thing's loss is another's gain

Other important observations are:
    Leaders hate to be alone, lonely, and disliked
    Violent people die violently

TAO TE CHING #43

The thoughtful person easily
Overcomes an angry one
Sometimes problems are resolved without action
And sometimes with the slightest action

A Tao Master teaches not by words
      But by non-action and subtle actions
      It is difficult to achieve this

TAO TE CHING #44

Which would you rather have
    Fame or good health?
Which do you value more
    Wealth or happiness?
Which is worse
    Success or failure?

The more you depend on others
    The less self-confidence you have
The more material things you acquire
    The less satisfaction you receive

Know when you have enough
    Otherwise you will not live in harmony
Fame, wealth, and success can be ok
    Only if you know when enough is enough

Moderation is the key to long life

TAO TE CHING #45

Success should be viewed with humility
A high position should not foster arrogance

Be straightforward with others
    But critical of yourself
Work hard in your efforts
    But make it look easy
Avoid extremes and
    You will gain insights
Do not act rashly
    But rather with tranquility

Being peaceful and serene
    Is the way of the *Tao*

TAO TE CHING #46

When people follow the *Tao*
    Even thoroughbred horses' dung is useful
When people do not follow the *Tao*
    The thoroughbreds are mated with draft
  horses

Conflict arises when people go hungry
It also arises when people want too much

So therefore learn when enough is enough
And there will always be enough

TAO TE CHING #47

Without going outside of yourself
    You can begin to be aware of the natural
  order
Without seeing outside of yourself
    You can begin to recognize the Tao within
  you

But on the path of life the more you understand
    The more you will realize you don't
  understand

So the Taoist is knowledgeable without going
    And recognizes without seeing
Thus achieving without having to take action

TAO TE CHING #48

When a person desires to know
    He accumulates something new each day
When a person follows the Tao
    He relinquishes a desire each day
    And continues to relinquish desires
    Until none are left

When no desires are left
    One does not need to take any action

The Taoist ideal is to observe the natural order
    Without the interference of one's desires
Intuitive knowledge is the preferred method

TAO TE CHING #49

A Taoist leader has an open mind
She is open to others' thoughts and ideas

A Taoist leader is kind to people who are kind
She is also kind to people who are not kind
For virtue (*Te*) is goodness

A Taoist leader is honest with people who are
    honest
She is also honest with people who are not honest
For virtue (*Te*) is honesty

A Taoist leader realizes that to combat
Aggression, hate, and anger is not with the same
But with care, consideration, and respect
Plus she treats everyone as her children

TAO TE CHING #50

The human body has 13 paths
Four appendages and nine apertures
These are the doors to senses and desires
Life and death pass through these gates

The key to longevity and
Resisting death is moderation

In order to build up a strong life force (*chi*)
Do not kill animals for sport
Do not use weapons of death on innocents

The *Tao* of the master is to benefit
Not bring harm to other living creatures

TAO TE CHING #51

The *Tao* creates all things in the universe
Its *Te* (power) nurtures them
Its natural law shapes and completes them

So all things without exception
Respect the *Tao* and worship its *Te*
Doing so without being commanded
But rather spontaneously

The *Tao* not only gives birth to all things
But also nourishes, cultivates, cares for, comforts,
    and protects
In the end taking each back into Itself

So the *Tao* produces but does not posses
Acts without any expectations
Guides without interfering
This is the wisdom of the *Tao*

TAO TE CHING #52

The Tao is Mother
Her children are all things
If you understand all things
You will understand the Mother
This will keep you from evil

If you control your desires
And keep from being judgmental
This will keep you from danger

If you are biased and prejudicial
And are greedy and dishonest
You will be susceptible to evil and danger

You must perceive the small things
    To gain awareness
You must know how to yield
    To gain strength
You must see inside yourself
    To gain insight

This is the path the Tao

TAO TE CHING #53

If one possessed even the slightest
    Amount of common sense
He would follow the path
    The Tao
His only reason to fear
    Is not following the path
The path is really pretty obvious
    But many tend to deviate

For example a bad government is
    Where buildings are excessive
    Farmers' fields have weeds
    The granaries are empty
    The royalty dress elegantly
    And they have to carry weapons
    They eat and drink to extremes
    And possess more wealth than needed
This is really stealing from the poor
And is not the way of the Tao

TAO TE CHING #54

Follow the *Tao*
Cultivate its ways
Not only will you find yourself at peace

But also the power of the *Tao* will bring
    Serenity to your soul
    Harmony to your home
    Unification to your community
    Freedom to your nation
    And calmness to the world

How do I know this?
By looking inside myself

TAO TE CHING #55

The Taoist is like a newborn child
>Whose bones are soft
>And muscles are weak
>But his grip is strong

While he does not yet know of human intercourse
>Yet his penis can be erect
>So intense is his *chi*

He can scream all day
>Without becoming hoarse
>Because he is in harmony with the *Tao*

So the Taoist must live in harmony
>To follow the *Tao*
He lives effortlessly
>Letting life flow without striving
He lives without struggling
>So he can be balanced
He is never disappointed
>So he can remain stable

Whatever is contrary to the *Tao*
>Will not endure

TAO TE CHING #56

A person who understands the Tao
    Does not boast about it
A person who boasts about following the Tao
    Does not follow the correct path

Therefore a Taoist lives in harmony by
    Listening rather than speaking
    Controlling his desires
    Not being judgmental of others
    Living simply
    Being humble

In being like the Tao you will
    Have an open mind to intuitive influences
    Become one with the ever evolving universe
    Gain personal power from self-knowledge

TAO TE CHING #57

Lead well by following the Tao
It helps to be unorthodox
It helps not to be bureaucratic
Your people will rise to the occasion

The more regulations you implement
    Your people will become rebellious
The more weapons a few people have
    The less secure all the people feel
If there are too many laws
    The result is too many criminals
Giving the people too many subsidies
    Makes them less self-reliant

So the Tao leader says
    If I trust the people more
        They will become more honest
    If I become less demanding
        The people are more relaxed
    If I do not manage the economy
        The people are more prosperous
    If I ignore influences
        The people become serene

TAO TE CHING #58

In a country governed with tolerance
    The populace prospers
In a country governed repressively
    The populace will rebel

Extremes never succeed in motivating people
    Try to make them idealistic results in the
opposite
    Try to make them happy results in misery
    Try to make them moral results in vice

The Tao leader governs by example
She is direct but not over-bearing
She is determined but compromises
She is charismatic yet simple

TAO TE CHING #59

In governing his citizens
A Taoist utilizes a leadership style of
Moderation, benevolence, righteousness
So the populace thrives

A Taoist leader accumulates power
So that nothing is impossible
He has the acceptance of the people
He leads effectively for their welfare

A government entity that is Tao centered
Can grow, prosper, and endure
It has a stable foundation
And can with-stand hardships

It is like a mother caring for her children

TAO TE CHING #60

When governing a country
It is like frying a fish
It is best not to disturb too much

With a Tao leader in charge
The dishonest people lose their power
While not all of them lose their hold over the
    innocent
It is just enough not to do harm

So the same with the Tao leader
Do no harm
This allows the citizens
The security to prosper

TAO TE CHING #61

With regard to the merging of two organizations
One large and the other small

The large one should be like a great river
Flowing slowly through all aspects of the new
    organization
The employees being humble and acting
    deferentially

The small organization should be respectful
Realizing its purpose is to be of service
Then it will not be over-powered

The large organization accomplishes its desire
    Of uniting and supporting everyone
While the smaller organization accomplishes its
    desire
        To join and serve more people

So both gain trust and cooperation
But remember it is always best
For the great to be humble

TAO TE CHING #62

The Tao is many things
A treasure for followers
Even a refuge for non-believers

Using praise for encouragement
Gaining respect for good example
Even helping those who are struggling
Because is it not right to help everyone?

An example, at the installation of a president
Or the promotion of vice-presidents
Let others offer jewelry or money
It is better to offer the Tao

Why did past Tao masters esteem the Tao?
Because when you are one with the Tao
    When you seek, you find
    When you err, you are forgiven
That is why the Tao is a treasure

TAO TE CHING #63

Act by not taking unnecessary actions
Work without needless effort
Taste without excessive savoring
Raise the lowly individuals
Increase the minority peoples
Above all repay bad acts with kindness

When it is easy, handle the difficult
Solving small problems prevent big ones
Little actions create gigantic tasks

So the Taoist lives wisely
In anticipating large problems
By accomplishing small successes
Thus achieving greatness

TAO TE CHING #64

A still object is easy to hold
Planning is easy at the beginning
A fragile ornament easily breaks
Small sand is easily scattered
So solve problems before they get big
And organize things before confusion

Remember a giant tree grows from a seedling
A tower is built on first laying one brick
A long journey starts with a single step

In rushing into action failure results
In grasping too many items all are lost

So a Taoist is thoughtful and
    Lets events take their course
She remains calm and careful both
    At the beginning and at the end
He who desires nothing
    Has nothing to lose
She learns best
    By listening
He encourages others
    To discover their inner-self

And thus they experience the *Tao*

TAO TE CHING #65

Taoist leaders are unknown as such
    By the general population
    Who tend to be unaware

However when a leader tries to be
    Too clever in his strategy
    The people will negatively react
A Taoist leader guides the people
    With simplicity and honesty
    Thus the population reacts positively

To know these things is to be
In harmony with the Tao

TAO TE CHING #66

Why is the sea king of all waters
Because all streams and rivers
Flow down to it

The same for a Tao ruler
He leads by putting his needs last
He speaks so everyone understands
He walks at the end of a parade

Remember if you want to be a good general
You must first be a good private
So the whole army identifies with you
And they do not feel oppressed nor manipulated

While the Tao leader is superior
He does not act superior

TAO TE CHING #67

Everyone thinks my *Tao* is universal
Which is why it is difficult to understand
This difficulty tends to make it unbelievable
If it were easy to comprehend
People would have discarded the idea long ago

I have three concepts to emphasize
Moderation, patience, compassion

With moderation you can be generous
But if you over-indulge
You have nothing to be generous with

With patience you can be thoughtful
But if you are aggressive
You lose seeing other options

With compassion you are able to see reality
As it opens your vision for others' situations
The *Tao* rewards the merciful

TAO TE CHING #68

A Tao leader does not use force
A Tao fighter does not get angry
A Tao master is not aggressive
A Tao employer is humble

This is called the power of composure
This is called the strength of compassion
This is called the harmony of the natural order

TAO TE CHING #69

Tao military strategists like to
>   Be patient and plan rather than be aggressive
>   Retreat when prudent
>   To advance when advantageous

They call this
>   Marching forward without advancing
>   See the guns and not the cannons
>   Capturing the enemy without their knowledge
>   Using deception as a strategy

There is no greater calamity
>   Than to under-estimate your enemy
>   To do so is to lose the battle

When two great armies meet in battle
Victory goes to the one reluctant to fight

TAO TE CHING #70

My teachings are easy to hear
And easy to put into practice
Yet most will not understand them
And thus fail to practice them

My thoughts originate from the beginning of time
My actions originate from the beginning of man
Because most do not know themselves
They cannot understand the *Tao*

The few who do know the *Tao*
Wear the clock of simplicity
And have compassion in their heart

TAO TE CHING #71

People who know they do not know are wise
Those who think they know but do not are
    ignorant

Those who acknowledge their weaknesses are
    strong
Those who abuse their power are weak

The Taoist seeks wisdom and strength

TAO TE CHING #72

When a Tao leader delegates his authority
    His authority will increase
When a Tao leader respects his employees
    His employees will respect him
When a Tao leader accepts his employees
    He is accepted by them

A Taoist knows himself
    But is not arrogant
A Taoist loves himself
    But is not haughty

TAO TE CHING #73

There are two kinds of bravery
One is about being able to kill others
The other is about not killing others
Both can be beneficial or harmful

While there is evil in the world
Who knows why or what
Not even the Tao master

The Tao in Nature
    Achieves without striving
    Gets responses without speaking
    Attracts without summoning
    Obtains effectiveness without planning

Nature is universal
Nothing escapes its influence

TAO TE CHING #74

When the people do not fear death
Because they lost their freedom
How can a leader threaten with death?
Now when the people do fear death
And the leader can execute them
Who would dare not conform?

Always there is a leader who can order executions
Which is violation of the natural order
So he is like a carpenter who saws
But rarely escapes some sort of injury

TAO TE CHING #75

The people go hungry
    Because leaders impose burdensome taxes

The people are rebellious
    Because leaders are too controlling

The people make light of death
    Because their lives are so difficult

On the other hand Tao leaders respect the people
By following the natural order

TAO TE CHING #76

At birth we humans are soft and pliable
When dying we become stiff and rigid
Trees are the same, tender and flexible when
    young
But become brittle and dry as they die

A Taoist is in harmony with life
    When she is adaptable and receptive
She is in harmony with death
    When she is inflexible and hard

TAO TE CHING #77

The Tao reflects Nature like a stretched bow
The top bends down while the bottom goes
    upward
So it is balanced by reducing the excess pressure
And increases what is insufficient

The Tao works in Nature the same
For example, reducing over-populated species
And increasing lesser ones

Non-followers of the Tao do the opposite
They take the insufficient from the poor
And give it to the rich who already have too much

The Taoist acts without any expectations
She succeeds without taking credit
She does not think she is better than others

TAO TE CHING #78

Nothing in nature is quite like water
It can flow gently down a stream
Or destroy rocks in a flood
Understanding this is not easy
When the soft overcomes the hard
Or the flexible overcomes the rigid
Most people know these facts
But only a few really understand them

Now Tao leaders who
Accept responsibility for their employees
And do not blame them for misfortunes
Seem to be successful by acting paradoxically

TAO TE CHING #79

When a conflict is settled unfairly
Resentment will grow
Resulting in a future conflict

Both parties should negotiate wisely
For an agreement
Which will solve all problems
So there can be no one to blame

This Way (*Tao*) works the best
When the parties are compassionate
And respectful

TAO TE CHING #80

Five hundred years ago
In the small native villages
The residents are content
Each enjoys his or her work
And each is productive
The families feel safe in their homes
While they have boats and horses
There is no need to migrate
Although weapons of war exist
They have not been used in a long time
There is sufficient food and clothing
The rituals are joyful occasions
The people love life
They feel secure in hearing from the nearby
    villages
The dogs barking and roosters crowing
Everyone is intent on dying from old age
The people live simply in the natural world

TAO TE CHING #81

Truthful words are not eloquent
Eloquent words are not truthful
Honest men are not argumentative
Argumentative men are not honest
Wise men do not know everything
Men who know everything are not wise

Taoists do not accumulate things
The more he gives
The more he receives
The more he lives for others
The more satisfying his life

The Way of the Tao is to benefit
Not to harm
The Way of the Taoist is harmony
Not to contend

www.ingramcontent.com/pod-product-compliance
Lightning Source LLC
Chambersburg PA
CBHW060406050426
42449CB00009B/1919